Lessons from the Garden

Lessons from the Garden

A Collection of Poetry from Abba's Heart

KEZIA KARUNWI

RESOURCE *Publications* • Eugene, Oregon

LESSONS FROM THE GARDEN
A Collection of Poetry from Abba's Heart

Resource Publications
An Imprint of Wipf and Stock Publishers
199 W. 8th Ave., Suite 3
Eugene, OR 97401

www.wipfandstock.com

PAPERBACK ISBN: 979-8-3852-2175-2
HARDCOVER ISBN: 979-8-3852-2176-9
EBOOK ISBN: 979-8-3852-2177-6

09/10/24

"Those who sow their tears as seeds will reap a harvest with joyful shouts of glee. They may weep as they go out carrying their seed to sow, but they will return with joyful laughter and shouting with gladness as they bring back armloads of blessing and a harvest overflowing!"

PSALMS 126:5-6 TPT

Contents

My Reason My Jesus   1

LESSON #1

Rehoboth   7
Home   8
You Saved Me   9
/Baby Talk/ v: to babble   13
Children Of Glass   15
Calling   17
God of Thunder   20
Freedom   22

LESSON #2

The Storm   27
Waves   29
Heavy   30
Darkness   31
Ink   32
Potential   33
Lesson   34
Spring Time   36

LESSON #3

Isolation	39
My Cross	41
In My Image	43
Purity	45
Children of Sorrow	48
Ricochet	50
Returning	51

LESSON #4

Pain	55
Labour Pain	57
Femininity	59
Airbrushed Ampersands	60
Thief	63
Peace and Unity / Perversion and Unrest	68
Holy Spirit	70
Er's Error	72
Here and Alive	74
The Sojourner's Journey	77
Eden	78

LESSON #5

The Garden	81
Tears into Gardens	83
Praise	84
Holier than Thou	85
Ladders and Spirals	89
Unfit Workers	90
Lessons from the Garden	91

MY REASON MY JESUS

I wrote this book for freedom
to feel something
to heal.

I didn't rhyme
(at least not all the time)
I put paragraph

breaks wherever I want
I have never had a class on how to write the perfect words
to captivate the reader
the only reader was me

until Him.

I could write a thousand poems about Him
and then some more
He makes me feel like . . .

He
makes
me
feel.

My poetry is how I feel
she is a one-way ticket into my soul
and the fact that His eyes have gazed upon a tiny fraction of her?

of me?
unencumbered and free?

Free falling like that? without a safety net?
truth is
it scares me
but nothing scares me as I write
free from judgement

Like I said,

I wrote this book for freedom
To feel something
To heal.

Now the Lord
God had planted
a garden in
the east

Genesis 2:8

LESSON #1

REHOBOTH

"Abandoning that one, Isaac moved on and dug another well. This time there was no dispute over it, so Isaac named the place Rehoboth (which means "open space"), for he said, "At last the Lord has created enough space for us to prosper in this land."

Genesis 26:22 NLT

HOME

I long to find my home in scripture
To flip through the wafer-thin pages
That cover all ages
The theme that binds them in leather
Binds us together
From cover to cover
It's you, Abba
You cover us in love.

YOU SAVED ME

A girl dripping in insecurity
Her identity she handled carelessly
shoving the jigsaw in any
Empty space
Expecting life to break through
Tied up, held captive
Her calling limited by the capacity
of her imagination
Shackles looked like bangles
Handcuffs like healing
Death like a dance-floor
Drowning out the gospel
Tuning into the beat of her own drum

I remember all the times,
Eyes rolling back on the sofa from
all the lines.
Puff puff pass
As time passed by
Without me even saying "hi"
to the Most High
Staying high all the time was
the way I coped

Coke mixed in a cocktail of pills
Hanging out in an abandoned mill
I felt sober

So many nights before my heart had
synced up to the beat of the dance floor
As I hungrily groaned for more
Like I was sucking every last
drop of serotonin dry
As I knew
I was no longer able to generate it my

Self

Self-worth shattered,
A distorted view of who I was called to be
As I crawled along the ground on my belly
Balloon between my knees.
Watching its swirly patterns swirl
While the world was still
Hallucinating because of the pill
Left me in a trance, one glance
and I was fixed. . .
Shards of glass snapped into place
And I could see myself
Painfully heavier yet I had lost
my sparkle and gained emptiness
The glass shards began to shift and distort
In a frenzy I fought
to keep seeing myself
"I don't know who I am" I exclaimed and broke down
Others around me crowded around
tried to console me
as they told me
who they thought I was.

Trying to fit pieces of their jigsaw in mine
while they too were under the influence.

There's a reason they're called spirits.

As we bumped keys
We unlocked a portal for entities
To enter me,
My entire being convulsed to the beat
& I thought this was fun

Bondage to Build up to Breakthrough
My story laid out before me
Then you restored me
This is my favourite part
You set me apart
set my feet on a rock
& for that
For You
I worship. I praise.
I get baptised in your name
Thank-you Jesus
Amen.

On the 28th November 2021
God looked down on His daughter and said it was done.
The war had been won.
And I had overcome.
My story, much like the Prodigal Son
Is one I share freely because
My purpose means more to me than *my pride*

So my opaque heart must learn to be transparent
And I pray it becomes apparent
As I reveal my battle scars and pour out my heart
God *always* finishes what he starts.

/BABY TALK/ V: TO BABBLE

Something bizarre has happened
My timeline has shifted from birth to death
To death to life
Death is no longer a destination
But a doorstep
Into the abundant life my Father promised me

Life rewinds herself before my eyes
And finally
I open my mouth
To release a babe's first cry
Like the breaking of dawn
To new life

As a babe, I babble
Reminded of my ancestors of babel
Their desire to be near to you
Left them striving to bridge the gap between heaven & earth
With mere dust
That gap you closed in one fell swoop
When you declared
"It is finished"
You drew me close to your chest
Skin to skin
So, I could finally feel your heartbeat
Against my eardrum

Once we had to climb towers
& lower our limbs through roofs
To hear from you
Yet now I hear you, clearer than ever
In my bedroom
As the veil was torn
A new intimacy was born
Between you and me

Father and child
Saviour & saved

Days stretch across the skies
As we lie here in the garden
My heart on your chest
You whisper to me
"My child, it's time to walk"

As I place my feet in your footsteps
I'll never forget
The first time I babbled to you
In my bedroom.

CHILDREN OF GLASS

The nights where sleep evades me
And my eyes feel like blinds, open and drawn
I find myself on my knees talking to the Son
About the children of the dawn.

The children that feel like glass,
Seen through, overlooked,
Forcing themselves into tight spaces
In fear of taking up more
The children that isolate themselves
Becoming self-reliant at a tender age
Learned to glue their mouths shut in arts & crafts
Pens replace voices & on pages they dance

The children that grew up too fast
Wise beyond their years
The ones that were exposed to reality too early
Shaping and creating their deepest fears
Those that sat in silence
Absorbing the chaos like a sponge
To those children,
I see you
& You are always allowed to be young.

To those children,
We are one in the same
We're all grown up now

& We're ready to claim
The space we hindered ourselves from
We're taking centre stage
Don't be afraid
It's finally your turn
Let people around you watch and learn
What it looks like when your candle
Finally burns

CALLING

living in your calling
might take a while
it's like
being handed the keys to an empty building
creaking doors and broken windows
once eyes to a soul
that doesn't call this place home anymore

it's like
walking into unfamiliar spaces
dust clinging to chandeliers
& doorknobs of jade
praying to not succumb to jaded-ness
or complacency
bowing to the altar of possessions
she's on her knees
begging for a chance to be seen
she
sees her name in lights
& fights for relevancy
exchanging her perspective
For 30 seconds
of fame

much like Adam
when Eve he blamed
much like Esau when he stooped

so low, trading his birthright
for a bowl of stew
much like Cain when
his unpreparedness met God's wrath
& bred embarrassment
leading to rash decisions
picked up a stone and with precision
in one movement he
took his brother's life
& lost his vision

we are our brothers' keepers
but we are not keepers of time
we do not get to decide
how long a life resides
on this side of eternity
life is but a vapour
sealed in a box reading
"handle carefully"
yet we toss our boxes around
with one another
when we're done we leave the box in an attic until the summer
when it's time to get our hot girl on

while our calling lays forgotten, collecting dust
just like esau exchanging legacy for lust
of the eyes , our own broken windows
the owner of the new house
comes inside
He paid the price
He looks around

creaky floorboards
mahogany wood
& says
"it is good"

GOD OF THUNDER

I think one of God's favourite miracles to perform
Is changing the weather, stilling the storm
To make his children smile
He says "My Child, wait a while
Let your Father handle this
Let me hang my bow between the clouds of your cheeks
And dress lilies fashioning a crown for your head."

I stare star struck
As He deftly places bolts of lightning across the sky
So deaf ears can witness the might of his splendour
While blind eyes hear the rumbling roar of the thunder.

I wonder if a thunderclap
is the sound Jacob's hip made under God's mighty wrath

The rumbles of an earthquake
the residual sounds of Goliath's skull meeting God's earth

If moonlight beams hold memories
of when Mary's eyes first met
Her son. Her Saviour. Her Jesus.

If ripples in the water giggle
at the memory of the miracle of the fish multiplying in their
    midst

I wonder if reminders of our Creator's existence within his
    creation
are signs of the times He's smiled, excited for us to experience
The life he's been carefully curating for us
From the beginning.

FREEDOM

Long before He set the earth's foundations
He had us in mind
Who is man that he thinks so highly
To intertwine us into his resurrection life
The One who turned water into wine
Traded His life for mine
& I cannot find words big enough to describe
This love built on sacrifice

How do I begin to pen
The One who let me touch his hem
The hem of Him I call my friend
That hem of healing

Freedom courses through my veins
Because I know my saviour reigns
In his love, he won't let us remain the same

On that cross my saviour died
He gave up his Spirit so we could experience
What it means to truly be free
The same tree He breathed into existence
Weighed heavy on His bones
Along the dirt roads of Calvary
Fashioned into a cross
I now carry on a silver chain

A reminder of the day
He broke mine.

LESSON #2

THE STORM

"But soon a fierce storm came up. High waves were breaking into
the boat, and it began to fill with water. Jesus was sleeping at
the back of the boat with his head on a cushion. The disciples
woke him up, shouting,

"Teacher, don't you care that *we're going to drown*?"

Mark 4:37–38 NLT

You are a garden fountain, a well of flowing water streaming down from Lebanon

Songs of Solomon 4:15

WAVES

When the waves of life
Come crashing in on my shores
May I be sure
That the One who set the boundaries of the ocean
Will protect me
May I know
That the one who holds the earth in his hands
Hears my cry
And may I have the courage to believe
He cries with me.

HEAVY

Life got really heavy
Too heavy
& I kept trying to silence the storm on my own
But life doesn't have a noise cancelling mode
No magic button I could press to repress the emotions
Bubbling beneath the surface
In an attempt to save face
I smiled "I'm fine thank you and you?"
If only you knew.

DARKNESS

Some say to rebuke spirits in Jesus' Name
But with depression
When the Son says you are free unconditionally
Somehow a conditional tag gets attached to that statement
A tag reading "healthy"
Even though I know the church more resembles a hospital to a
    hotel
When you are constantly the patient it's hard to tell
If the doctors and nurses really mean well
Or behind your back they're airing all your details
To the other patients, snickering
Doctors bickering at your bill
Wondering how you're going to pay it,
Well Jesus—that's how
But a stitch there, a transplant there, next thing you know it's
    open heart surgery
& I thought I was free?
So why do I still need to rely
On this life machine.

INK

Joy is to be experienced through others
As if for a brief moment, what's theirs is mine
I dip my nib into their explosive pot of ink,
Pressing it to paper
Soaking up the vibrant strokes before my eyes
Reminding myself that this is what life is
If only, I could experience it myself
But for now, I'll enjoy the brief moments I get,
Watching others paint vibrant colours
With their lives
Waiting for the day,
I do the same.

POTENTIAL

I'd rather die while I still had time

time to

succeed

achieve

create

be celebrated

laugh

smile

dance

be

than to be remembered as

the girl that had potential

& didn't use it

I'd rather cease to exist

On the precipice

between

the prayer & the promise

LESSON

in school we learned
to sit cross legged
& recite our abc's
to learn our times tables
& pray on our knees
but somewhere along the lines
the ones we drew
& the ones we filed into
life grabbed hold of the chalk
embodied the blackboard
& began to talk

life spoke to us about
how to be liked
be kind
sit up straight
give great advice
shine your light
people will like you
people will do the same

but life was wrong
some people
are attracted to your light
like moths to a flame
but instead of trading love for love
they trade love for pain

they play table tennis with your heart
& string you along like a beaded necklace
they chew you up along with their food
& spit out the seeds
you lovingly sowed
all those years ago

so be still my heart
before you go leaping into another's hands
be prepared for these
modern games we play
ring-a-roses & hopscotch
were soft & plush
but gaslighting & microaggressions
are sharp and tough
piercing through my fleshy heart
before it even had the chance to start

SPRING TIME

I'm happy it's spring time for you
I'm happy the skies are blue
& change hues more gradually
Giving you time to bask in the light
Without fear of the dark thoughts creeping in

I'm happy it's spring time for you
Where the flowers bloom
Gracing us with their tapestry of colours
Our very own rainbows on the ground
I'm happy the earth showing off her beauty
Gives you the courage to do the same

I pray one day, even while the sky isn't bubblegum blue
& the clouds aren't cotton-candy pink
While the world is still frozen over, in hibernation
And darkness seems to be winning
I pray you see the beauty in just being
Knowing that displaying your wonder is beautiful
But you my love, are wonderful, full in every season.

For Julie

LESSON #3

ISOLATION

The son said to him, "Father, I have sinned against heaven and
against you. I am no longer worthy to be called your son."
But the father said to his servants, "Quick! Bring the best robe and
put it on him. Put a ring on his finger and sandals on his feet."

Luke 15:21–22

they will build
houses and dwell
in them; they
will plant
vineyards and
eat their fruit

Isaiah 65:21

MY CROSS

I took off my cross necklace today

I stopped carrying my cross
The symbol of my saviour's love
Bearing what was my debt to pay

Its silver chain once shone brilliantly against my sepia-toned skin

Now it buckled beneath the weight of the truth it bore

Rusted and weary from exposure to the elements
As I unclasped the worn chain

I exchanged one belief for another

I replaced the cross with a pendant "K"

Fashioned in my image

Looped through a string of pearls, cheaply bought

With an inbuilt affinity for swine.

"It's only temporary" I lied
I'll put it back on tonight
A couple of hours became days, weeks and then months.

As time stretched,
the distance between my heart and the Father's
grew with it.

What was once found, proudly worn on the crest of my heart

Was now lost, forgotten and falling apart.

IN MY IMAGE

You say you do not worship it
Yet you find your worth in it
Palming pretty crystals between the creases and calluses of your
  palm
This couldn't possibly be doing harm
Right?
Writing and reciting incantations masked as affirmations
Biblical blessings without the inclusion of Christ are nothing but
  blasphemous blight
Dictating your future in futile attempts to control
Your story God has already foretold

Still you pay a pretty penny for the pendant around your neck
Pensive and perspiring awaiting what's next
Tapping on the tarot cards telling. . .
Tricking you into a false sense of reality
Turning to creation not the Creator for a semblance of sanity.
Creating idols out of gold that cannot see
Nor hear
Nor know
Your story God has already foretold

Astrology makes a mockery of the identity God has placed in
  thee
Replacing what's anointed with a falsehood of what it is meant to
  me
Paying for palmistry to predict your progeny
Yet the Psalms tell you He knows before they are even born

Idolatry comes in many different forms
Attempting to withhold
Your story God has already foretold

I leave you with a question
Will you surrender from this quest?
Understanding God knows best?
And leave the rest
To Him
Who counts every hair on your head?
The stars you look to
He calls by name
His thoughts of you outnumber the grains
of sand

Will you, take hold of his hand
And let him direct you
Let His Word be a light unto your feet
And a lamp unto your path
Leave your striving in the past

And be still and know He is God.

PURITY

We get excited about marriages
But we don't care what marriage is to God
We love the instagrammable moments
And the fanfare
But don't even realise
That the Holy One is not there
The decor and fanfare are all good
Except when they take over the place God once stood
The Heavenly one in our midst

Purity is a matter of the heart
That is where it starts
External parts
We use to help us abstain
Will not claim
Or retain
The gift that God has given
That will sustain us
Until the end

Purity is our friend
Not our foe
We do not need to fight
With bow and arrow
To retain it
However, God wants us to refrain
From crossing the boundaries

That He so carefully set for thee
To maintain our purity

We are children of the Most High
Bought with a price
So when the price is not paid in full
Down payments lay in the hands of fools
Pigs taking pearls and expecting the world to applaud
When in reality, we need to pause
reflect on what brought us here

Only in Abba's arms are we called to draw near
The further we run from His design
The harder it is to hear his reminder of the truth
We were bought with a price
When that price is not right
When that price is not paid
Before the day we lay with our spouse
Then the blessings of God will not cover
The multitudes of our sin
Only then do we discover
The mess we are in
We make a fool of a holy and whole God
We mock our maker when we mistake
Magic Mike moments for miracles

This poem may feel lyrical
But it is spiritual
Reminding you that until you say 'I do'
You are still seen as two
The two will not become one

Until the one who said 'It is done'
Says it is done

So until the marriage of the lamb,
When we are reunited both old and young
We cry holy, holy, holy
Joining in the angel's song.

CHILDREN OF SORROW

Ears sensitive to a pin drop
Trained to hear the difference between anger and joy
Through a stair creak
Through a tone in an adult's speech
That would decide their entire week

They learned early
That they shouldn't speak so clearly
On the matters of their heart
Muffled mumbles mentioned in a moment : A mantra

The ones who knew it was better to hide
Than be wild
Better to a shrinking violet
Than a social butterfly
To be a peace-maker
Than an extrovert

Children of sorrow
Grow into
Anxious adults
Unlearning the early years
Unsafety ushered us into undulating unhappiness

A choice needs to be made
A line in the sand
Maintain the status quo
Or take a stand

RICOCHET

'You dodged a bullet'
a popular phrase
when you hold resentment for someone
and a friend tries to compensate your pain
but
they never think
What if I didn't want to dodge it?
what if I wanted to burrow myself deep within the chaos
making my home
marking my territory
calling him mine
until our souls are so intertwined
I no longer know where mine stops and his begins
what if I never dodged a bullet
but
became it instead

RETURNING

Your touch feels foreign to me
Like a lover who has forgotten
How to be loved
My skin has grown tough stretched and expanded
Over the increasing time spent away from you
Impregnating me with doubt
& giving birth to
The distance between us

You call for me
And I cower
Expecting lashings and responsibility
I do not have the strength
To bear
Yet you draw me near
And I can't ignore your voice
The sweet familiarity albeit losing its pungency
Traces of honey still remain laced to your kind words
& that is enough
To make me turn my head
Change my mind
My heart still remains inclined to you
Abba

I'm ashamed to admit I've turned to other lovers to warm your
  seat
But nothing and nobody can compare to the warmth I feel when
  I fall at your feet
I'm reminded of the joy in your presence
And ask you take residence
On the throne of my heart
Once again.

Abba,
I'm back home.

LESSON #4

PAIN

"For his anger lasts only a moment,
but his favour lasts a lifetime!
Weeping may last through the night,
but joy comes with the morning."

Psalms 30:5

It is like a
mustard seed
which a man took
and planted in
his garden. It
grew and became
a tree, and the
birds perched in
its branches.

Luke 13:19

LABOUR PAIN

A labour of love
Planted itself deep within me
Claiming my vessel as home
Inconspicuous and unannounced
Yet its presence grabbed the mic of my heart
And began to speak out in the dark
Cries in the wilderness of my womb, formerly barren and stark

Almost like your arrival in my depths incited warnings from the
    heavens
Lest you be mistreated, aborted before time
Requiring terms & conditions
You know? Like the kind we often skip
So quick to rush to the check mark
That we forfeit the fine print
If only I had stopped to further inspect the white spaces and
    black lines
I would realise I was missing the in between
Of the promise and the delivery
The grey area preceding the victory

See I was promised a new thing
Excited to hold you in my arms
Bounce you on my knees
Revelling in the joy and accomplishment you bring
Never once did I doubt the seed deposited inside of me
Would bring forth a bountiful replenishment of His investment

But

Nobody warned me to prepare for your delivery

I was so wrapped up in your love

I neglected the impact of your pain

Ripping me from the comfort I grew accustomed to

Tossing and turning in familiar spaces that no longer brought
  comfort

Pricking fingers on pins while I stitched

Fig leaves together to hide our nakedness

Embarrassed to admit my failure to prepare to bear your
  greatness

Now, your due date is here

& I am unprepared

FEMININITY

I'm beginning to harden
The chrysalis I was in went into crisis
As the creases in my cheek turned into cracks
I began to harden
The garden withered away
When Eve chose fruit over faith
And man's true ambition lay bare, full display

My softness stripped away
By a man in a boy's frame
Playing house with mine
This is not the game I wanted to play

AIRBRUSHED AMPERSANDS

Define womanhood

According to Google it is "the state of being a woman"

I thought using the same word you're defining while describing
  its purpose was forbidden

Womanhood: a collective of women

(There we go again)

This word so hard to source, almost like a diamond mine

Except everyone wants us to believe we're peanuts, they don't
  want us to shine

Only good to be spread when a man's in a jam

Viewing us in slices of whiteness

Never whole & complete

Woman AND is not allowed unless your "and" meets

Society's standard: woman and white

Anything else sets of fight or flight

Fight: argue that feminism cannot be intersectional otherwise the
  definition falls like a pack of cards

Flight: look away, terminate, eject and discard

Who knew it would be this hard

To define what a woman is

Womanhood

The qualities that seem to be natural to or characteristic to a woman

Hidden, precious gems lie at the root of its origin

From homemaking to girl bossing to foraging

Outdated and truncated expressions of femininity

Distract from the distinct divinity

God bestowed upon us when we were made in his image

Distortion through the mirror of conditions has me reeling
A woman's "meaning" certainly has no ceiling
Yet society wants to put a cheap cap on our glass vessels
Shake us around & say we're only worth our milkshake
& then shame us for it

Then if a woman decides to go corporate
She's made a caricature of her character
Say she's bossy rude and loud
In an attempt to embarrass her
If she chooses to settle down and have kids
A privilege she may have the chance to give
Abdomen or adoption the love stays the same
Her privilege is still stripped away
By boys playing men in suits
Casting lots on women's bodies when it suits them

It seems like women are stuck
Between a rock and a hard place
But we know we can't be replaced
The men that want to erase us
Have a woman's eyes, in the hollows of their face
They hold a woman's smile between their cheeks
But what they are too weak to hold
Is a woman's cries who was once at peace
When she is made to feel ravaged and cheap
Left in pieces

*Men force milk down their throats from glass bottles that never
wanted their caps off
& get away scot-free*

While she lays there, her body now being sold as meat
To the highest bidder, or anyone that will take a peek
& you ask her not to be bitter
But to stay sweet

Until one day she meets a man
He doesn't take advantage, she thinks he might understand
He says to her, "Talitha Koum"
Daughter stand
I saw you in your mother's womb
Don't you understand
I designed you to be bold and soft
Assertive and nurturing
Lion and lamb
Just like me
Don't you see, womanhood cannot be defined by a phrase or
    three
Let me teach you, let's go back to Eden
Take my hand,
I'll give you a reason
To believe again
I'll bring you your freedom
To receive again

Let's start at the very beginning
A very good place to start

THIEF

See I thought we were being honest here

Because honesty is the best policy

I politely declined your invitation to intertwine your thighs with
mine

But you prescribed your remedy regardless

Took no regard to my no's or the tears burning holes through my
cheeks

You had your way

Now it's time for me to have mine

How dare you take advantage of my innocence & inebriation

For years I blamed myself, maybe I showed hesitation or
resignation

Did I even say no

But no

Non verbal cues are still not a green light

For 5 years I've been fighting on your side

But tonight? Tonight I'm snatching the trophy from your sight

Tonight the power of God inside me is reminding me that this is
not by my might

But by the Spirit of God beckoning me to be the voice for the
voiceless

I am here to remind you that

It wasn't your fault

You didn't drink too much

You didn't seem too interested

My love, stop gaslighting yourself

Because when that gas meets the embers of your fragile heart

And lights, that spark? That spark becomes a forest fire within seconds

Burning up everything you've built yourself to be

Can't you see? You are the physical embodiment of beauty from ashes

Ashes that have been passed back and forth

And shaken off by unworthy hands

One day you'll learn to dance

Without fearing the rain

One month you'll take a chance

On love again

One year you'll look back and realise

All you see in the mirror are your eyes

Dry and bright

Because weeping may endure for a night

But joy comes in the morning

For now you might be mourning

Your inner self

Her innocence, her freedom

That little girl a victim of man's selfish ambition

You are allowed time to process

Your emotions are like camera film roll

Delicate, impressionable, need time to develop

So it's okay if it's dark for a little while during your development season

But promise me you'll let the light in soon?

Promise me,

You won't leave those emotions hanging by the cloth pegs of self-contempt for so long

That you forget how it felt when that camera first went "click"

Pick the narrow path
The road less travelled some may call it
The one that forces you to unload your heavy burden
Take another yoke instead
It's lighter anyway

Leave your pain in the arms of the one who endured the cross for
  you

He is not cross with you
Or judging you
Or upset with you
He loves you
He adores you
He will restore you
& adorn you with jewels

because you are *precious* to Him

If you want to know more about this Him I speak of
You'll find Him in between the lines of your primary school
  hymns
You'll find Him deep down in the pile of fake news about
  religiosity
Between the lines of suffering in this world
You'll find Him in the hope
in the shores as he set the moon to draw in their tides
So we too can reside on this planet
Coexisting with the fish

You'll find Him in every breath that you take

Selah

A reminder that you are not a mistake

And it is His breath that gives you life every day

Selah

When you look for Him
You'll find Him
I'll give you a clue
His name is Jesus

Some of you here may get a sick feeling in your stomach hearing
    that name
Maybe you haven't heard it since those primary school hymns
Maybe there have been too many hims since him
That have hurt you, taken advantage
That from your vantage point
Me asking you to add another him to heal you makes you ques-
    tion my intelligence
Or maybe you're on the fence
Used to living life on defence
All I will say is take a chance
You might just learn to dance again
Without fear of the rain

In Mark 5:41
This "Him I speak of"
Said two words to me that bought my freedom Talitha Koum

"Little girl, stand up"
That pain shut up in your bones does nothing but keep you in
   bondage
So pour out your weary soul
Unclench your jaw
Lower your fists
Stand up
& step away

This is God's battle now
if that is okay?

PEACE AND UNITY /
PERVERSION AND UNREST

I have no longing left in my lungs for my land
I have no hope left in my heart for her healing
Rulers lead with an iron fist
Pedestrians on pebbled paths persistently petrified
Our terrain turbulently toiled by terrifying tyrants

Sọ̀rọ̀ sókè screams the soil of my land

                Silence

The blood of our brothers beneath us beckoning for
   breakthrough

              They are silenced

Weeping widows war with wailing

                Silence

The diaspora desperately desires our destiny to be different

              We are silenced

People are patiently parched persistently pleading with patriarchal
   parties to pay attention

                Silence

Graphite and rubber
The difference between
Great leadership and rebellion
The truth and a lie
How many more lives need to lie before you
Until you hear our cries

I pray for *the day*
Our silence becomes deafening
The day
Compliance becomes defending
The day
The longing for my land returns to my lungs.

HOLY SPIRIT

But now I am going away
And you grieve
You grieve not only because I leave
But the trees don't seem as green
Without me here to guide you
You grieve because you have walked alongside me obediently
Following my every step
& now it is your turn
To practise what you have learned at my feet
Remembering to always wash one another's
Through my departure I pray you discover
That I am truly omnipresent

I will send an advocate
One who will take you under his wing
And teach you, turning your trials and temptations into testimonies
I will send an advocate
An encourager who will anchor you in my truth
Who rejoices in your youth
Reminding you it's okay to be childlike

I will send a guide
Who will remind you of my teachings
And empower you to live by them
Who will discipline you in love when you've gone astray
Because he would leave the 99 every day
If it meant, he had you.

I will send a teacher
Who crosses all your t's and dots all your i's
When you don't have the strength to disguise the pain in your
    eyes
Who groans on your behalf
When you are half empty
Reminding you that his power is plentiful enough to replenish
    your weary soul

I will send a friend
Who will hold your hand till the very end
Reminding you of everything I've said
When the waters He once hovered over
Find their home in the brim of your eyes
He will hold a bottle up to your tears
Capturing them as they caress your cheek
Each drop a reminder of the years
You have walked in step with me

My child,
Will you accept Him?
Will you accept me?
Or will you remain fixated on milk
& neglect meat
I long for you to grow strong in faith and understanding
Which is why I no longer stand here
But trust me my child
I am always with you.

ER'S ERROR

I wonder what Er did (Gen 38:7)
The error that Er erred
That stirred God's holy anger
To strike him dead

As I read this passage at 3am
I began again
Thanking God for His hem
The hem of him I call my friend
That hem of healing

Instead of striking us at our errors
He entrusts us with his arrows (2 Kings 13:8)
Reminding us that if only we had struck the ground more
Total victory would be ours

What strikes me every time
Is the coexistence of God's judgement and his generosity
In His love, He leaves no animosity
Between man and Him
Yet in his judgement His love still shows
As he cannot go against the words He chose
Each word serves as a plank of wood
In the picket fence of protection
Around God's chosen ones

So in reality, when God says no
He's protecting us
In his grace he remembers that we are made from only dust
Incapable of escaping powers like lust
On our own
He tells us to flee
He shows us we are free
Our feet now function obediently
Away from shackles

So on days where I wonder what Er did
His error I use as a mirror
Taking the log from my eye
Before I even begin to wonder why
God struck Er dead
Because it was probably for something
I've once said.

HERE AND ALIVE

You see me
5ft 8 and plus-sized
& label me "unhealthy"
What you don't see

Is the history

The time I politely declined his invitation to intertwine his thighs
    with mine
& he didn't hear me say no
You don't remember all the times my eyes rolled back on the sofa
    from all the lines
Puff puff pass as time past by
You don't know my ears are sensitive to a pin drop
As they were trained to hear the difference between anger and joy
    through a stair creak
Through a tone in an adult's speech
That would decide my entire week

The body keeps the score
Three nil to me & the crowd wants an encore
I'm often overwhelmed by the voices within

But then I remember him

Him who told me I was only pretty when I was thin
Watched as I twirled on the grimy club floor

& told me
I only deserved love if I fit a size twelve

Him who told me I looked better without my glasses
I told him he did too

Them who screamed at me "orobo"
When I only wanted to get my hair done
I was five years old

I remember her
Who in her native Korean tongue told me I was fat in Year 8
That night I cried on Google Translate
That day was the last day I cleared my plate
Dinners after that consisted of soup
Lunches—jacket potato skins
And for breakfast I heaved my sins of the night before
Four am binges leaving my self respect hanging on its hinges.

I remember it *all*

& I look at myself today—mascara streaked face
I remind her that she is okay
She made it, yes she's not a size 6
But at least she's not 6 feet under ground

Fix your crown
You're fat and alive
Wipe your frown
You don't have to cry

Look around
You're here and alive

Life tried to end you
Multiple times
But Jesus saved you
& you're here and alive

To the reader,
Next time you want to tell someone what they already know
Consider the history, that you may not be shown.

THE SOJOURNER'S JOURNEY

One month I was Jonah, coaxing the jaws of the
fish open, seeking solace & security in its bowels.

The next I was Peter, cautiously watching the
jowls of the rooster reverberate as I drove the
third nail into the depths of my deceit.

Then I was Balaam, eyes rounded in disbelief as
the mouth of an ass made a caricature of my lofty
confidence, its feet crushing the inflated ego
smugly sat on the throne in my chest.

Until eventually, my avoidance caught up to my reality
Placing my calloused feet
in the calf-skinned sandals of the Prodigal Son

I rerouted my journey back home
Returning to the One.

EDEN

Restoration bursts her way through
The barren landscapes of my heart
Threading her way through the cracked, tear stained earth
Singing her song as she works
"Revival is here
The time is now
Let dry lands find hope
Let dead vines revive
The time is now"
She hovers over the dry lands
And remembers the waters
Beckoning to my spirit
Come alive
The time is now
Eden has found a new home
In your heart.

LESSON #5

THE GARDEN

"I went down to the grove of walnut trees
and out to the valley to see the new spring growth,
to see whether the grapevines had budded
or the pomegranates were in bloom."

Song of Solomon 6:11 NLT

he will make
her deserts
like Eden

Isaiah 51:3

TEARS INTO GARDENS

A familiar stinging in the back of my eyes
Signifies the breaking open of the well
The well I sit at every day, unassuming
Pouring my heart out into the darkness
Until one day,
I have a visitor.
A man, feet clad in calf skin shoes
Skin bronzed by heritage and blessed by the sun
It is clear to me that this visitor is special
Wiping my eyes, I turn to gaze at him
He tells me
"My child, you've been here for a while
See how your tears have watered the grounds around you"
I cock my head, puzzled.
Until I shift my focus from the darkness of the well to the path
    surrounding.
Once barren and dusty now covered in lush greenery, ripe and
    ready for harvest
My Visitor begins again
"Your land is ready for harvest my child,
Just as I promised
Your pain has a purpose"
In that moment I recognized My Visitor's voice
I reply
"Abba, look what we did
We made a garden"

PRAISE

Mellifluous praise poured out of my heart
Pooling at the base of my throat
Entwining itself around my languid larynx
Like a mother, stirring her child into alertness after an afternoon
    snooze
Before her release into the world,
She made up part of my DNA
Ingrained in my purines and pyrimidines
Was a desire to praise

Every nerve in my body was aware of the arrival of her song
Every cell debriefed of her importance
My organs stood at attention
It was almost as if
As if my entire being
Was acutely aware
It was created,

Created to praise.

HOLIER THAN THOU

The English Dictionary is not extensive enough
No gift is expensive enough
To unveil the glory of the Most High
So He came down,
the greatest DIY in history.

As a storyteller is to a story
I am a humble servant to my creator readily reflecting His glory
A puppet to the greatest ventriloquist in existence
How I love His persistence
He breathed one breath in me and I'm a real boy
Yet I turn to idols to pull my strings
Then act surprised when through me they sing

I give my voice away
To Yahweh, the one who deserves my praise
May every breath in my lungs
Every word on my tongue
Profess the name of Jesus
The King of Kings that never leaves us
El Shaddai Almighty God
Crafted me carefully in my mother's womb
Wrapped himself in flesh only to be held in a tomb
The tomb meant to cage Him became a cocoon for His
    transfiguration
His power can alter all situations
His power sets on fire generation after generation

The one that with words woke up the world
Rejoices over you in singing
The one that spoke the sun into shining
Counts every hair on your head
The one that separated seas from the skies
Knows you by name
How great is our God?
That he humbled himself
Came down into the very world He made
To save us, as a helpless babe.

Yet I do not praise Him for the flowers, but I praise Him for the
    roots
I cannot despise the humble beginnings because they are the
    origins of my youth
As Jeremiah said Blessed is the man who trusts in the Lord
Not for any reward
But to be planted by living waters
Roots buried deep beneath the surface
Connected to the vine
Pruned and purified perfectly designed
For his purpose, planted.

You see, the world promises band aids for bullet wounds
Temporary fixes that leave you addicted
To the beat of the wrong drum
In your own strength you strive to become
a saviour of a war He's already won

That plaster by the way, it's peeling off
Revealing the cracks in the unfired clay

Those imperfections you tried to bandage
God never wanted you to manage
He is the potter and you are the clay
Let him mould you and pass you through fires
That He promises will never burn you
Instead will turn you into a reflection of himself.
He is the surgeon and you are the patient
Let Him patiently take you through the surgery of sanctification
While you bow before him on your knees
How long will you surrender?
To let Him render holiness in you
El Roi
God who sees you
Will see to it that He sees His likeness through you

Until the Day our saviour returns
Not as a babe this time
But a warrior, trading the donkey for a horse of white
Behold, the mighty return of the Word of God
From His mouth comes a sharp sword
In the beginning was the Word
And the Word was with God
Then the Word was with us
And the Word never returns void
So the revenant will return for the remnant
Eyes blazing with all glory
Victorious over the evil one

Until that day comes
When we are transfigured with Christ
New bodies, restored life

Will you stay in the cocoon?
Let him transform you
through His Word
Let the Holy One make us
Holy too.

LADDERS AND SPIRALS

Life is not a ladder, it's a spiral
Some may see spiralling as a bad thing
But I see it as learning
Ladders leave no space for mistakes
As it's always about the next rung
A step down means you're further from your destination
& closer to where you've come from

Spirals encourage growth
Beginning in the middle you make your way outwards
Each turn reflective of a new lesson
You know more than you did then so this time it's different
Although experiences might feel familiar
The difference is in the lessons you've learned
Looking back at previous turns
You have two options
You can either return to your old way of doing things
Or learn from the past

& turn your spiral—into a spring

UNFIT WORKERS

There is not enough space
Between the words on this page
To encapsulate
Your g l o r y
Yet you entrust our hands
That cannot hold all of you
To enter the garden you made,
We tend the soil,
So, the buttercups sing
"holy holy holy"

All creation joins
In the song of our hearts
Our eyes fixed on you
Only you.

LESSONS FROM THE GARDEN

Dear reader, thank you for journeying with us, Abba & I
Now it is time to say goodbye.
I think the beginning is not only a good place to start
But a great place to end.
Let's go back and recite our ABC's, my dearest friend.

A sapiens seed
plants himself in the hollows of your heart

Born from lauded lashings
and crucifixion

Colloquially called "A sapiens' sacrifice"
this heart beat of history
tore the veil
broke the seal
between living waters
and dry streams

Dormancy interpreted as death yet
beneath the surface the complexities

Extinguish the belief
that waiting equates to inactivity

Far from the soil
his seed extends itself
gracing the plains of your terrain

Growth; an indication of healing
yet pain intertwines herself in the process
birthing her sister, wisdom

His humble healing
through his seed
better described through
anthropomorphism
or transubstantiation
depending on your beliefs

I Am that I Am
wrapped Himself in flesh
cocooned Himself in the tomb
deposited Himself in your heart

Juxtaposed light and darkness
holiness and sin
coexist in the conditions of your soil
a choice stands before you
death or life
these two idols can no longer mix
choose life

Kingship forfeited
in a Bethlehem babe's first cry
teaches you to wail in weakness
not suffer in silence

Leaves break onto the surface
as the waters that broke the seal
break open his seed
deposited in thee

Meandering through the maze of your
heart
His waves whisper songs
His voice, echoes of rushing waters

Night encapsulated in the light
landscapes shining in His glory
history repeats itself
unveiling mysteries before thee

Ordered steps
reminding you that
an iota of intentionality
breeds a bounty of mustard-seed blessings

Processes from purpose to produce
punctuate the picture
deposition to
dormancy to
development to
delight

Quickly, the tides change
formerly hidden victories
erupt from the soil into the skies

Reaching outward
to reach hearts
announcing to other plants around
there's a journey to embark

Start with Jesus
start today
journey with friends
and don't be afraid

The bark He bled on
broke the chains around your feet
so you can embark on this journey
your soul continuously at his feet

Under grace, this race of faith
is to be run with conviction
knowing that your seed
is surely within the process
of germination

Value the time of dormancy
the sower intimately tending to his seed
his deposit, a down payment of your destiny
bridging the gap between
the Father and thee

Wait expectantly
signs of growth may ebb and flow
thorns may threaten to choke the roots
but remember whose soil you are growing in
& breathe in knowing you can rest in Him

XXX—XXXIII
show that God never delays
30 years of perceived dormancy
bore 3 years of miraculous activity
proving the personal process
precedes the public victory

Your story may be found in pieces of my words
fragments of my heart might resemble puzzle pieces of your path.
For that, I praise God.
May your weary soul find solace in the similarity
but remember we are called to gather for strength
and scatter to share our light and individuality.
So promise me, you won't get so comfortable in these pages
that you forget the wages paid to break the shackles around your
    feet
you're free now, rejoice, go out there
& dance in the rain
help others learn
there's a purpose to their pain.

Zero fear, zero doubt
the garden gates are open,
you, fellow sojourner have journeyed well

I'll see you soon
& you'll know my Father has spoken.

Not the End. Until He says so.

Milton Keynes UK
Ingram Content Group UK Ltd.
UKHW031306141024
2172UKWH00003B/4